**ENJOY** every day.

COMPENDIUM™
PUBLISHING

live inspired.

There's a good
time coming.

SIR WALTER SCOTT

ENJOY every day.

The moments of
happiness we enjoy
take us by surprise.
It is not that we
seize them, but
that they seize us.

ASHLEY MONTAGU

**ENJOY** every day.

Joy rises in
me, like as a
summer's morn.

SAMUEL TAYLOR COLERIDGE

ENJOY every day.

Embrace the
ordinary with
enchantment.

YOLA PERKINS

**ENJOY** every day.

Things are only
worth what one
makes them worth.

MOLIÈRE

ENJOY every day.

Life is not a
stress rehearsal.

LORETTA LAROCHE

**ENJOY** every day.

Time you enjoy
wasting, was
not wasted.

JOHN LENNON

**ENJOY** every day.

Let us go singing
as far as we go.

VIRGIL

ENJOY every day.

We live in a
beautiful world.

**ENJOY** every day.

All day, where
the sunlight played
on the seashore,
Life sat.

OLIVE SCHREINER

**ENJOY** every day.

Capture the moment,
whoever you are.
None of us is here
forever.

ANNABELLE REDDING

**ENJOY** every day.

Sing away sorrow,
cast away care.

MIGUEL DE CERVANTES

**ENJOY** every day.

On some days,
a shade tree
and a few minutes
can change your
whole attitude.

UNKNOWN

**ENJOY** every day.

My heart is like
a singing bird.

CHRISTINA ROSSETTI

**ENJOY** every day.

Live in the sunshine,
swim the sea, drink
the wild air...

RALPH WALDO EMERSON

**ENJOY** every day.

The cure for boredom
is curiosity. There is
no cure for curiosity.

ELLEN PARR

**ENJOY** every day.

In the long run, the
pessimist may be
proved to be right,
but the optimist
has a better time
on the trip.

DANIEL L. REARDON

ENJOY every day.

If people never did
silly things nothing
intelligent would
ever get done.

LUDWIG WITTGENSTEIN

**ENJOY** every day.

If you want to keep
your memories,
you first have to
live them.

BOB DYLAN

**ENJOY** every day.

I wish I could stand
on a busy corner,
hat in hand, and
beg people to
throw me all their
wasted hours.

BERNARD BERENSON

**ENJOY** every day.

I have enjoyed
life a lot more by
saying yes than
by saying no.

RICHARD BRANSON

**ENJOY** every day.

Seek wonder in
the ordinary,
and miracles will
happen that you
cannot explain.

SARAH N. RAND

**ENJOY** every day.

Expand your capacity
to be delighted.

UNKNOWN

ENJOY every day.

The world is your
playground. Why
aren't you playing?

ELLIE KATZ

**ENJOY** every day.

First things
first, second
things never.

SHIRLEY CONRAN

**ENJOY** every day.

Joy is not in
things, it is in us.

J. HOLLAND

**ENJOY** every day.

It's the little
moments that
make life big.

KOBI YAMADA

ENJOY every day.

The essence
of pleasure is
spontaneity.

GERMAINE GREER

**ENJOY** every day.

Never pass up an
opportunity to have
a Popsicle with a
four-year-old.

JOHN P. SMITH

**ENJOY** every day.

To all upon my way,
day after day, let
me be joy, be hope.
Let my life sing!

MARY CAROLYN DAVIES

**ENJOY** every day.

This day is a
journey, this
very moment
an adventure.

REBECCA PAVLENKO

**ENJOY** every day.

The greatest of
all miracles is
to be alive.

THICH NHAT HANH

**ENJOY** every day.

Why not seize
pleasure at once?
How often is
happiness destroyed
by preparation,
foolish preparation!

JANE AUSTEN

**ENJOY** every day.

To love and be
loved—this on earth
is the highest bliss.

HEINRICH HEINE

**ENJOY** every day.

Happiness is not in
our circumstances,
but in ourselves.
It is not something
we see, like a
rainbow, or feel,
like the heat of a
fire. Happiness is
something we are.

JOHN B. SHEERIN

ENJOY every day.

Unshared joy is an
unlighted candle.

SPANISH PROVERB

ENJOY every day.

Stop every now
and then. Just stop
and enjoy. Take a
deep breath. Relax
and take in the
abundance of life.

UNKNOWN

Delight in
the beauty that
surrounds you.

UNKNOWN

**ENJOY** every day.

Climb the mountains
and get their good
tidings. Nature's
peace will flow into
you as sunshine flows
into trees. The winds
will blow their own
freshness into you,
and the storms their
energy, while cares
will drop away from
you like the leaves
of Autumn.

JOHN MUIR

**ENJOY** every day.

How many times
have you noticed
that it's the little
quiet moments in
the midst of life
that seem to give
the rest extra-
special meaning?

FRED ROGERS

**ENJOY** every day.

I think it annoys
God if you walk
by the color purple
in a field and
don't notice.

ALICE WALKER

**ENJOY** every day.

We are all
wanderers on this
earth. Our hearts
are full of wonder,
and our souls are
deep with dreams.

GYPSY PROVERB

ENJOY every day.

Journeys. Even the word sounds as if it has been drawn from some magic elixir and distilled through the gossamer screen of the imagination.

PHYLLIS TAYLOR PLANKA

ENJOY every day.

A person who
is looking for
something doesn't
travel very fast.

E.B. WHITE

**ENJOY** every day.

A heart in love
with beauty never
grows old.

TURKISH PROVERB

**ENJOY** every day.

I go to nature to
be soothed and
healed, and to
have my senses
put in order.

JOHN BURROUGHS

ENJOY every day.

Now and then
it's good to pause
in our pursuit of
happiness and
just be happy.

ANONYMOUS

**ENJOY** every day.

There are books in
which the footnotes
or comments scrawled
by some reader's
hand in the margin
are more interesting
than the text. The
world is one of
these books.

GEORGE SANTAYANA

**ENJOY** every day.

It's never too
late—never too
late to start over,
never too late
to be happy.

JANE FONDA

ENJOY every day.

Many people
miss their share
of happiness,
not because they
never found it,
but because they
did not stop to
enjoy it.

WILLIAM FEATHER

ENJOY every day.

The universe is full
of magical things,
patiently waiting
for our wits to
grow sharper.

EDEN PHILLPOTTS

**ENJOY** every day.

The world is grand,
awfully big and
astonishingly beautiful,
frequently thrilling.

DOROTHY KILGALLEN

ENJOY every day.

Life is not a journey
to the grave, with the
intention of arriving
safely in a pretty
and well preserved
body, but rather to
skid in broadside,
thoroughly used up,
totally worn out, and
loudly proclaiming,
"Wow! What a ride!"

UNKNOWN

**ENJOY** every day.

Right now a
moment of time
is passing by! ...
We must become
that moment.

PAUL CEZANNE

**ENJOY** every day.

Life, even in
the hardest times,
is full of moments
to savor. They
will not come this
way again, not
in this way.

PAULA RINEHART

**ENJOY** every day.

Be happiness itself.

BUDDHA

**ENJOY** every day.

The wise don't
expect to find life
worth living: they
make it that way.

UNKNOWN

**ENJOY** every day.

Go to the window
and look at the stars.

RALPH WALDO EMERSON

**ENJOY** every day.

The human
heart yearns for
the beautiful.

HARRIET BEECHER STOWE

**ENJOY** every day.

When I slow down
long enough to
smell the roses,
I usually see the
beauty and all
else that is ours
to share.

MORGAN JENNINGS

ENJOY every day.

A happy person
is not a person in
a certain set of
circumstances, but
rather a person
with a certain
set of attitudes.

HUGH DOWNS

**ENJOY** every day.

Adventures are to
the adventurous.

BENJAMIN DISRAELI

**ENJOY** every day.

If we live good
lives, the times
are also good.
As we are, such
are the times.

ST. AUGUSTINE

**ENJOY** every day.

It is one life,
whether we
spend it laughing
or weeping.

LISA SPIELMAN

**ENJOY** every day.

The days come and
go, but they say
nothing, and if we
do not use the gifts
they bring, they
carry them as
silently away.

RALPH WALDO EMERSON

ENJOY every day.

Not what we have,
but what we enjoy,
constitutes our
abundance.

JOHN PETIT-SENN

**ENJOY** every day.

One never knows
what each day is
going to bring. The
important thing
is to be open and
ready for it.

HENRY MOORE

ENJOY every day.

You live longer
once you realize
that any time spent
being unhappy
is wasted.

RUTH E. RENKL

**ENJOY** every day.

Rest is not idleness,
and to lie sometimes
on the grass under
the trees on a summer's
day, listening to the
murmur of water, or
watching the clouds
float across the sky
is by no means a
waste of time.

SIR J. LUBBOCK

**ENJOY** every day.

If something's
important to you,
you make time for it.

MIA MAESTRO

ENJOY every day.

If I thought things
would no longer be,
I would have tried
to remember better.

KOBI YAMADA

**ENJOY** every day.

The happiness of life
is made up of little
things—a smile, a
helping hand, a
caring heart, a word
of praise, a moment
of shared laughter.
We are most alive
in those moments
when our hearts
are conscious of
our treasures.

THORNTON WILDER

**ENJOY** every day.

The only way to
live is to accept
each minute as
an unrepeatable
miracle, which is
exactly what it
is—a miracle and
unrepeatable.

MARGARET STORM JAMESON

ENJOY every day.

If you can have just a little fun today, it's a sign that maybe the future will hold even more fun for you. Fun isn't just fun—it's hope.

LINDA RICHMAN

ENJOY every day.

Just living is not
enough, said the
butterfly. One must
have sunshine, freedom,
and a little flower.

HANS CHRISTIAN ANDERSEN

**ENJOY** every day.

Living itself, [is] a
task of such immediacy,
variety, beauty, and
excitement that one
is powerless to resist
its wild embrace.

E.B. WHITE

ENJOY every day.

Does the day
belong to you or
do you belong
to the day?

LEE IBEN

**ENJOY** every day.

Time has fallen
asleep in the
afternoon sunshine.

ALEXANDER SMITH

**ENJOY** every day.

And those who were
seen dancing were
thought to be insane
by those who could
not hear the music.

FRIEDRICH NIETZSCHE

**ENJOY** every day.

Life is the movie
you see through
your own eyes.
It makes little
difference what's
happening out
there. It's how you
take it that counts.

DENIS WAITLEY

**ENJOY** every day.

Cheerfulness is
the atmosphere
in which all
things thrive.

NORMAN DOUGLAS

ENJOY every day.

At the height
of laughter, the
universe is flung into
a kaleidoscope of
new possibilities.

JEAN HOUSTON

**ENJOY** every day.

The most beautiful
thing under the
sun is being
under the sun.

CHRISTA WOLF

**ENJOY** every day.

The priority in life
is the quality of
life...day after
day after day.

WATSON KENNEDY

ENJOY every day.

Go forth into the
busy world and love
it. Interest yourself
in its life, mingle
kindly with its joys
and sorrows.

RALPH WALDO EMERSON

**ENJOY** every day.

Mingle a little folly
with your wisdom;
a little nonsense
now and then is
pleasant.

CARMINA HORACE

**ENJOY** every day.

How true it is
that what we really
see day by day
depends less on the
objects and scenes
before our eyes
than on the eyes
themselves and the
minds and hearts
that use them.

F.D. HUNTINGTON

ENJOY every day.

I have found that
sitting in a place
where you have
never sat before
can be inspiring.

DODIE SMITH

**ENJOY** every day.

Nobody can
conceive or imagine
all the wonders
there are unseen
and unseeable in
the world.

FRANCIS P. CHURCH

**ENJOY** every day.

Where there is
laughter there is
always more health
than sickness.

PHYLLIS BOTTOME

**ENJOY** every day.

The only thing that
has to be finished
by next Tuesday is
next Monday.

JENNIFER YANE

**ENJOY** every day.

How precious
everything would
seem...if we knew
that today was
all we had.

ALAN CLEMENTS

ENJOY every day.

Remember the
feeling as a child
when you woke
up and morning
smiled? It's time
you felt like
you did then.

PETER TORK

ENJOY every day.

You have a gift that
only you can give
the world—that's the
whole reason you're
on the planet. Use
your precious energy
to build a magnificent
life that really is
attainable. The miracle
of your existence
calls for celebration
every day.

OPRAH WINFREY

ENJOY every day.

If you spend your
whole life waiting
for the storm,
you'll never enjoy
the sunshine.

MORRIS WEST

**ENJOY** every day.

If your capacity
to acquire has
outstripped your
capacity to enjoy,
you are on the way
to the scrap heap.

GLEN BUCK

**ENJOY** every day.

My happiness
is not the means
to any end. It is
the end. It is its
own goal. It is
its own purpose.

AYN RAND

ENJOY every day.

That time was like
never, and like
always. So we go
there, where
nothing is waiting;
we find everything
waiting there.

PABLO NERUDA

**ENJOY** every day.

Gladly accept
the gifts of the
present hour.

HORACE

**ENJOY** every day.

In the time of
your life—Live!

WILLIAM SHAKESPEARE

**ENJOY** every day.

Every joy is gain,
and gain is gain
however small.

ROBERT BROWNING

**ENJOY** every day.

I am open to
receive with every
breath I breathe.

MICHAEL SUN

**ENJOY** every day.

You, whose day it is,
get out your rainbow
colors and make it
beautiful.

TRADITIONAL NOOTKA SONG

**ENJOY** every day.

There is precious little
hope to be got out
of whatever keeps us
industrious, but there
is a chance for us
whenever we cease
work and become
stargazers.

H.M. TOMLINSON

**ENJOY** every day.

May we always
have old memories
and young hopes.

LOREN ADAMS

ENJOY every day.

And through and
over everything,
a sense of glad
awakening.

EDNA ST. VINCENT MILLAY

**ENJOY** every day.

Earth and heaven
are in us.

MAHATMA GANDHI

**ENJOY** every day.

No road is long
with good company.

PROVERB

**ENJOY** every day.

Gratitude before
me and behind me.
Gratitude to the
left of me and the
right of me.
Gratitude above
and below me.
Gratitude within
and all around me.

ANGELES ARRIEN

**ENJOY** every day.

I still find each
day too short for
all the thoughts I
want to think, all
the walks I want
to take, and all
the friends I
want to see.

JOHN BURROUGHS